Dinosaur Whodunnit?

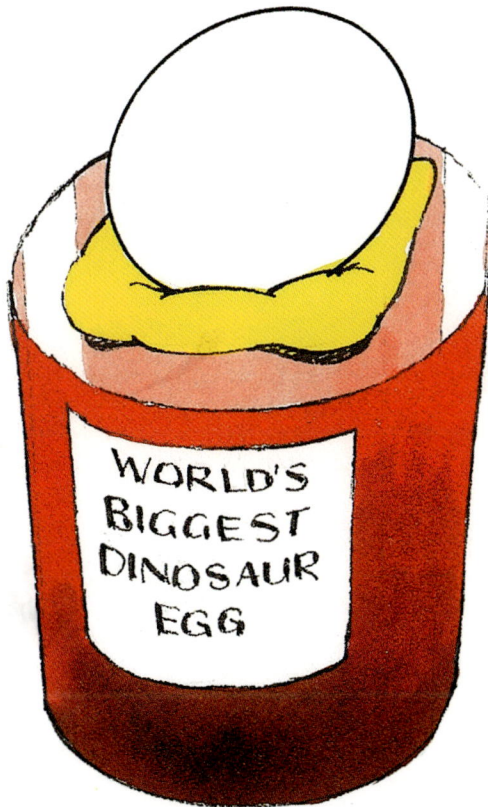

WORLD'S BIGGEST DINOSAUR EGG

Written by Jane Langford
Illustrated by David Mostyn
Adapted by Jane Moates for the
Heinemann English Readers series

Heinemann

Heinemann Educational Publishers
Halley Court, Jordan Hill, Oxford OX2 8EJ

An imprint of Harcourt Education Limited
Heinemann is a registered trademark of Harcourt Education Limited.

Literacy World Satellites edition © Jane Langford 2000
Heinemann English Readers edition © Jane Langford, Harcourt Education Limited 2006

10 09 08 07 06
10 9 8 7 6 5 4 3 2 1

British Library Cataloguing in Publication Data is available from the British Library on request.

ISBN 0435 294601 / 978 0435 294601

Designed by Nicola Kenwood @ Hakoona Matata Designs
Illustrated by David Mostyn

Cover design by Nicola Kenwood @ Hakoona Matata Designs
Cover illustration by David Mostyn

Printed and bound in Malaysia by Vivar

Acknowledgements
Every effort has been made to contact copyright holders of material reproduced in this book. Any
omissions will be rectified in subsequent printings if notice is given to the publishers.

Contents

Key words

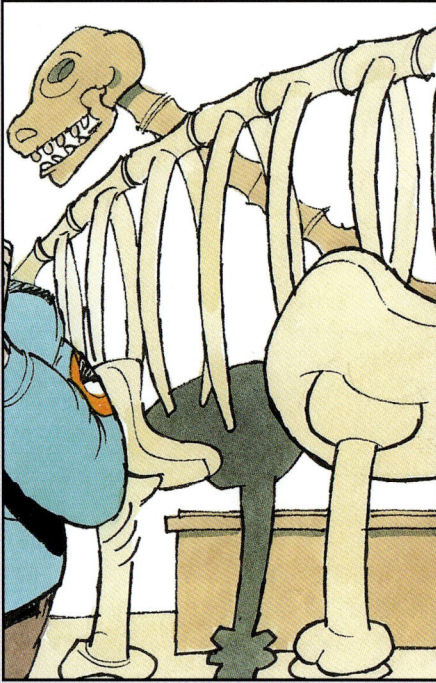

dinosaur skeleton

museum

exhibition

dinosaur

a whodunnit

detective

security man

alarm

clue

mayor

egg

WORLD'S BIGGEST DINOSAUR EGG

security lights

CHAPTER ONE

Tom and Mollie run up the steps of the museum. Today is the first day of the dinosaur exhibition.

The lady at the desk speaks to Tom and Mollie.

Tom and Mollie go in. A man wearing sunglasses goes in after them.

-an / -ian
an American is a person from America
a Malaysian is a person from Malaysia

The lady at the desk picks up the telephone.

Hello, security?

That man wearing the sunglasses is here again.

I'll watch him.

Tom and Mollie look at the dinosaurs.

Look at those teeth!

All the better to eat you with!

The security man looks at the man wearing the sunglasses.

Here again, Sir?

Yes, I really like museums.

10

plurals
one tooth / two teeth
one foot / two feet

Tom and Mollie like the dinosaurs.

Look, he's got me!

PUT YOUR HEAD IN HERE.

PHOTOS £2

Ha, ha, ha!

The security man doesn't like the man touching the dinosaurs.

Can't you read?

DO NOT TOUCH

like / don't like
I like dinosaurs. I don't like spiders.
She likes dinosaurs. She doesn't like snakes.

A lot of people push past Tom and Mollie.

Stand back for the Mayor!

Excuse me!

The people go into a little room.
Tom and Mollie follow them.

SPECIAL EXHIBIT

Where are they all going?

excuse me
Excuse me, may I ask you to move back?
Excuse me, what time is it?

The security man follows the man wearing the sunglasses into the little room.

Quiet please.

SPECIAL EXHIBIT

What's in there?

I don't know.

special: very important
Your birthday is a special day.
He wears special boots for playing football.

A TV man points his camera at a big case. The case is in the middle of the room and lots of people are looking at it.

Is it a dinosaur?

I don't know! It's got a big cloth over it.

I know / I don't know
I know how to spell my name. I don't know how to spell your name.

The Mayor starts to speak.

Today is the first day of our dinosaur exhibition. It is also the first time that people can see ...

THIS!

She punches in a secret code ...

$100 = a hundred dollars
$1 000 = a thousand dollars
$1 000 000 = a million dollars

CHAPTER TWO

The Mayor starts to speak again.

You may take photographs, but please do not touch.

The case is protected by security lights and by our security man.

commands
Do not touch! Sit down! Stay back!

The people push forward to see the dinosaur egg.

The TV man is pushed into the Mayor.

The Mayor is pushed into Mollie.

careful: with special care, in a gentle way

Mollie is pushed into the security lights.

Oops!

Red lights flash. Alarm bells ring.

Oh, no!

That's the alarm!

exclamations
Oops! I dropped the egg.
Oh no! That's the alarm.

A second security man comes running into the little room.

Get up!

Hold her!

The security man is very angry.

I will have to turn off the alarm system now!

I'm sorry.

But you were pushed.

to turn off
It's time for bed. Turn off your computer.
It's too noisy. Please turn off the music.

The security man takes a key out of his pocket.

I'll turn this.

Will it turn off the red lights?

Yes.

And will the alarm bells stop ringing?

Yes.

questions and answers with 'will'
Will we see dinosaurs at the exhibition? Yes, we will.
Will that switch turn the computer off? Yes, it will.

The security man turns the key. The red lights stop flashing. And the alarm bells stop ringing.

Phew!

That's better!

But then ...

then: after that

The lights have gone out!

Help!

Mollie is scared. So is Tom.

What's happening?

I don't know.

to scare: to give someone a fright or to become afraid

Someone speaks.

Stand still!

SECURITY

I will turn the lights back on.

Mollie feels someone push past her.

Ouch! Who scratched me?

someone: a person
to scratch: to make lines or cuts using something sharp, such as nails

Suddenly the lights come on. The dinosaur egg is missing! The man wearing the sunglasses is not in the room.

CHAPTER THREE

Tom and Mollie look at the empty case.

Where is the egg?

I don't know!

Who took the egg?

TOILETS

empty: not having anything inside

The security man looks at Tom and Mollie.

Tom and Mollie are very scared. Everyone is looking at them.

We didn't take it.

TOILETS

Suddenly the Mayor screams.

Oh no! Where's my bag?

everyone: all the people

What was in it?

The Mayor thinks for a minute.

Umm. My lunch was in my bag.

But I ate my lunch. So the bag was empty.

past tense
What was in it?   My lunch was in my bag.
The bag was empty.

29

thief: someone that steals something

How did you know that?

Because you were the ones who did it!

So where have you put the egg?

And where have you put my bag?

who
You were the ones who did it.
You know who was there.

We didn't take the egg.

I think you did.

No, we didn't!

Then Mollie has an idea.

I know! Look at the film in the camera.

Yes! That will show us who the thief is!

TOILETS

idea: a thought or plan about something to do
film: material used for recording photographs

dark: when there is no light
The opposite of dark is **light**; the energy from the sun or a lamp that lets us see things.

The security man looks at Tom and Mollie.

I still think it was you.

He takes them out to the desk.

Ring the police!

But we didn't take the dinosaur egg.

to ring: to telephone

Then Mollie sees something that gives her an idea.
Suddenly she shouts.

I know who did it!

So do I!

But do you?
Go on, guess whodunnit!

Read and remember

Read these questions and try to answer them from your memory. (In some of the activities that follow, the first question has been done to help you.)

1 What is the name of Mollie's friend? (*Tom.*)

2 What was the name of the dinosaur Mollie wants to see?

3 Who was looking at a newspaper?

4 Who was eating a chocolate bar?

5 Was the man with the sunglasses wearing a hat?

6 What was the colour of the security man's shirt?

7 What colour was the dinosaur egg?

8 Who turned the alarm off?

9 Who pushed Mollie into the security lights?

10 What colour was the mayor's bag?

Digging deeper

1 To be a good detective, you must be able to find information. Look at these signs from the museum. Find what page they are on and then write the signs in full.

Dinosaur _____

Do ___ touch

World's biggest _____ egg

_____ £2

Special _____

2 Find the newspaper page in the book. Read the information below and check if it is correct. Write the newspaper page correctly.

The Post

Australian offers £11,000 for world's smallest egg.

Comparatives and superlatives

Read these sentences and then think about the rule below.

The Tyrannosaurus Rex is **bigger** than the Compsognathus.
The Compsognathus is **smaller** than the Tyrannosaurus Rex.

To compare two people or things add –er to the end of the adjective.

Think about the rule above and write sentences comparing the sizes of these dinosaurs, using the words given in brackets.

1

   Tyrannosaurus Rex   Diplodocus   (big)

2   

   Compsognathus   Tyrannosaurus Rex   (small)

3   

   Compsognathus   Tyrannosaurus Rex   (tall)

4

   Diplodocus   Tyrannosaurus Rex   (long)

5

   Tyrannosaurus Rex   Compsognathus   (short)

6   

   Compsognathus   Tyrannosaurus Rex   (big)

Notes for teachers and parents

Background

1 This book is a simple 'whodunnit' detective story that introduces the topic of dinosaurs. Discuss the story and ask the students to tell you about the clues in the story. Ask them if they have read or seen any other detective stories. Encourage them to find other detective stories to read or watch.

2 Discuss with the students what makes a good detective. Encourage them to think about the skills of observing carefully, remembering facts and thinking carefully.

3 Ask the students to read the story again and find as many adjectives as they can. Ask them to write a list of these adjectives and to add any other adjectives they know. Finally, ask the students to use a dictionary to check their work.

4 Ask the students to read the story again and find as many adjectives as they can. Ask them to make a chart showing the present and past tense of these verbs. The students can then sort the verbs into regular and irregular verbs. Encourage them to add any other verbs they know. Finally, encourage the students to use a dictionary to check their work.

5 Encourage the students to look for signs in English in their environment and write them down. These may include anything from stop signs on the road to the names of shops. The students can make a collection of signs and share them with their friends.

How to get the most out of this book

1 It is helpful if the students can read the book in pairs, reading one page aloud each. Reading aloud should help with recall and it also encourages the students to understand and remember words and phrases.

2 Encourage the students to look at the key words pages before reading the rest of the book. These pages are designed to be used as a picture glossary. It is also helpful to have an English dictionary available for the students to use.

3 The coloured strips at the bottom of each page show the language used in the text in either a different way or a different context, or may help introduce a new word. Looking at these will help the students to better understand the text and to develop their English.

Answers

Read and remember

1 Tom
2 Tyrannosaurus Rex
3 the lady at the desk
4 the lady at the desk
5 yes
6 blue
7 white
8 the security man
9 the mayor
10 red

Digging deeper

1 Dinosaur exhibition (pages 7 and 8)
  Photos £2 (page 11)
  Do not touch (page 11)
  Special exhibit (page 12 and 13)
  World's biggest dinosaur egg (page 16)
2 American offers £1,000,000 reward for world's biggest egg.

Comparatives and superlatives

1 The Diplodocus is bigger than the Tyrannosaurus Rex.
2 The Compsognathus is smaller than the Tyrannosaurus Rex.
3 The Tyrannosaurus Rex is taller than the Compsognathus.
4 The Diplodocus is longer than the Tyrannosaurus Rex.
5 The Compsognathus is shorter than the Tyrannosaurus Rex.
6 The Tyrannosaurus Rex is bigger than the Compsognathus.